YOU BEGIN WITH LANGUAGE

You Begin *with* Language

Master the Foundation of **HUMAN EXPERIENCE**

Nathan Max Osorio

EMEGIR
MEDIA

Copyright © 2025 Emegir Media LLC
All rights reserved.

You Begin with Language
Master the Foundation of Human Experience

First Edition

ISBN 978-1-5445-4778-7 *Hardcover*
       978-1-5445-4777-0 *Paperback*
       978-1-5445-4779-4 *Ebook*

To my sons, Nathan Michael Osorio and Noah Rupert Osorio. You are my greatest teachers.

Contents

INTRODUCTION 9

1. IMPORTANCE OF LANGUAGE 15

2. STEP 1: RECEIVING THE MESSAGE 27

3. STEP 2: PROCESSING AND CONTEXT 39

4. STEP 3: RESPOND 59

5. THE ACT OF CREATION 73

CONCLUSION 91

ACKNOWLEDGMENTS 95

ABOUT THE AUTHOR 97

Introduction

In January 2012, while undergoing chemotherapy for his Stage 4 lung cancer, my father caught a cold and never recovered. Doctors hospitalized him and induced a coma because he needed intubation to receive sufficient oxygen. Liquid filled his lungs, and doctors could not remove it; medication was ineffective. As he passed away, I promised my father I would take care of everything, he didn't need to worry, and he could rest now.

I was twenty-six years old with a little more than a year of being a licensed attorney and with less than a year of owning my law office. Still, I promised I would take care of the family. I would be the patriarch from now on.

I did not make that promise in a vacuum. My father was Peruvian and very sexist—a *machista* as we would call it in Spanish. So even though I have a sister six years my elder, my father envisioned me taking over his business.

As his male heir, I was raised being called *licenciado* by his staff and clients, a term of respect loosely applied to a professional. But by the time I was twelve, I had decided I did not want to be my father. Why? My dad was a workaholic. He loved being at the office. He also loved taking part in groups that praised him. He was never around much for me. Add that to a very messy and traumatic relationship he had with my mother, which led to their separation when I was about nine years old, and needless to say, I did not like the person my father was.

I never wanted to sit at my father's desk, running his business, yet I promised I would take care of everything when he passed. Why? Because I was a dutiful son. I loved my father and my family. And at twenty-six years old, knowing that my grandfather was a womanizer and an alcoholic, that both my grandparents died when my father was a young teen, I appreciated what he had accomplished in his business as an immigrant to the United States. I appreciated how he treated everyone who came through his doors with respect and dignity.

Have you ever done anything begrudgingly? Why do you think that is? Where did your underlying disdain and anger come from?

For ten years, I managed my father's business with the constant thought of, *I am not and will not be my father.* Business was stable, but money was always tight because I knew little about running a business successfully. My workload and stress levels were excessive, and like many on this planet, I had little hope or inspiration for the future. I existed to provide for my family and raise my kids, and that's it.

During the COVID-19 pandemic, I viewed the closure in Los Angeles as an opportunity to finally leave law and get my real estate license. I thought, *If I can find joy in some other work, then I'll be happy.* Sound familiar?

By 2022, I felt disorganized and stuck, as well as limited in what I could practice. While I enjoyed helping families obtain lawful status, my work was colored by the thought that I didn't want to be my father. Yet it wasn't until I began my personal development journey that I truly realized I was surviving, not living.

Personal development doesn't fix anything; it allows space for things to be revealed. It allows space for you to inquire, explore, and ultimately choose. And we do all this with language. At the core of personal development is the effective utilization of language: receiving, processing, and responding to messages, whether they're our own thoughts, others' statements, or the written word.

Every person on this planet uses language. As babies, we use our bodies and fingers to indicate what we want. Our parents applaud our first words, but the continued acquisition of vocabulary and grammar quickly overshadows them. The first time we play tag with our friends and say, "You're it," the first time we say, "Stop it," to our annoying classmates, the first "Mine" claiming an object as our own—these are not special moments for any of us. We've said so many things since then; you've probably said many things today before even opening this book!

Language is wholly mundane for us. That a person can learn and speak a language with all its phonology (sounds), morphology (word formation), syntax (sentence structure), semantics (meaning), and pragmatics (contextual use) is wondrous, but we aren't amazed by it at all. In fact, we learn languages so effectively that it does not surprise us when someone knows two or three of them, each with its own complex rules for speech, writing, and gestures.

Yet language is much like water to us. Intellectually, we know we need water—our brain is 95 percent water, lungs 90 percent, blood 83 percent, bones 22 percent. Many of us have spent too much time in the sun without water and felt refreshed and healthy after drinking a lot to recover. The eight-glasses-a-day advice codifies the importance of water for our organism to operate. However, we largely forget water as an essential ingredient.

The key difference between water and language, for our purposes, is that language has no physicality to it, ever. You can't grab language up and feel it flow through your hand like sand. It won't hit you in the face like a rock thrown at you. It also won't cause you to drown like water or push you down like a hundred-mile-per-hour gust of wind. Anything we hear, say, or read gets processed in our minds, but we react as if it has a physical impact on us. Our bodies tense. Our teeth clench. Our fists close.

Humans have no experiences like those with language. An "I don't love you anymore" from a partner of ten years can make your breathing stop and your mind go blank like you're having a panic attack. The greatest speeches in the world can touch souls and ignite passions, rallying thousands of people. But language is just a means of delivering a message.

What negative messages do you hear from society, your community, strangers, loved ones, or yourself? How has your processing of those messages impacted your words and actions? Can you hear any message and not have an instant reaction? Can you respond to a message with freedom and ease and not with frustration, justification, and judgment?

This book is not the culmination of my life's work; it is a snapshot of the personal development journey I started in 2022. By tracking my thoughts and communications, I've learned that when language is graspable, it's malleable. When you break down your internal and external messages—what is said, what it meant, and how you're reacting to it—you can choose new ways of thinking and communicating.

For me, this meant choosing my father's business as it was and as it wasn't. Once I chose it, other possible choices appeared. I chose special education law after advocating for my sons who have autism. I chose to develop a coaching program and write this book for those, like me, who want a new tool set to engage with life in a powerful and intentional way. And I will continue to choose.

Thank you for choosing this book. May it empower you to keep choosing.

CHAPTER 1

Importance of Language

The bigness of language struck me when I read *Sapiens* by Yuval Noah Harari. My personal development journey was well on its way, and I used the tools I had to work through the issues that arose in my life. *Sapiens* opened a door for me where I later discovered Steven Pinker and similar scholars.

Before we can effectively utilize language, we must experience the phenomenon of language as distinct from our use of it. Having language fundamentally changes our relationship to the world. Our development of language took place over tens of thousands of years in a world that no longer exists. It is this evolution of language that enables us to be the dominant species on this planet and paralyzes us with anxiety and fear of judgment from others. The proceeding is largely based on *Sapiens* by Yuval Noah Harari.

All human beings alive today are members of the species *Homo sapiens*. Around 150,000 years ago, sapiens thrived in East Africa, but we were not the only members of the genus

Homo that populated the planet. Until around 50,000 years ago, four other species of humans roamed the planet at the same time: *Homo sapiens* (us), *Homo erectus, Homo neanderthalensis* (Neanderthals), *Denisova hominins* (Denisovans), and *Homo floresiensis* (hobbit-sized humans). So what happened between 150,000 and 50,000 years ago that left us as the only human species around? About 70,000 years ago, *Homo sapiens* left Africa and began spreading across Asia and Europe and the rest of the world until only *Homo sapiens* remained. Interestingly, around 100,000 years ago, *Homo sapiens* attempted to enter Neanderthal territory, but they failed. We don't know the exact reasons, but 30,000 years later, nothing could stop *Homo sapiens'* dominance. So what changed?

The cognitive revolution occurred. Yuval Noah Harari states that between 70,000 and 30,000 years ago the emergence of boats, oil lamps, bows and arrows, needles (needed to sew warm clothes), and art occurred. The first evidence of religion, commerce, and social stratification is shown here. Researchers say that the species that could do these things are as intelligent, creative, and sensitive as we are. We could break bread with them, learn their languages, and exchange ideas.

So why is this important? Our species existed for hundreds of thousands of years before the cognitive revolution. We had domesticated fire, which led to cooking, which changed how much food we needed to eat, how much time it took to get that food, and how long it took to digest. Some scholars believe this directly led to the enlargement of our brains and the expansion of our faculty.

So we as a species existed well before the cognitive revolution. Once the revolution occurred, we, as a species, stood apart from the rest of the animal kingdom and other humans who roamed the earth. Within 20,000 years, we, *Homo sapi-*

ens, were the only human species on the planet. Why? Well, language, of course.

Other animals have types of language or ways of communication. For example, some monkeys have specific calls for dangers to warn others. There is a call for danger in the sky (eagle). There is a call for danger on the ground (lion). Some even make these calls to trick their brethren and steal their food. Language is also present in bees, ants, elephants, whales, parrots, and the list goes on. But our language is much more subtle. As Yuval explains, we can connect a limited number of sounds and signs to produce an infinite number of sentences, each with its own unique meaning. While a monkey could communicate, "Danger! A lion," a human can tell us that she saw a herd of bison near the bend in the river at a specific location. The vastness and complexity of our use of language, combined with our innate ability to learn, use, and create with it, sets us apart from all other species on our planet.

The main point of this trip down evolutionary biology lane is that we, as a species, have a capability like no other species that we know of. Language is in our genes, in our minds. Just as water is a building block of all life on earth, language is an essential part of every human being on this planet. It connects every one of us. We will see that when we don't have language, we yearn for it, and once we get it, we can't willingly revert to the experience without it.

LIVING WITHOUT LANGUAGE

As of this writing, my six-year-old son has a significant speech delay. His speech expression is limited to three- or four-word phrases about specific objects. For example, he may want more rice, but he calls it spaghetti. He knows both words but doesn't use them correctly all the time. While limited in expression, he understands many phrases. When we tell him to do something, he has appropriate reactions, showing his understanding and ability to comply with our requests. Language is still fundamental to his experience as a human.

Most people have no concept of being without language. Try to imagine it and describe it. Guess what. You are using language to get a grasp on it. You have no context for this experience if you've never existed without language. We must look at the experiences of those who existed without language and later obtained it. Those who remember their existence before language acquisition.

At nineteen months old, Helen Keller lost her sight and hearing due to illness. She never regained them. When she was six years old, a teacher began working with her, and she began to acquire language, leading to her becoming an author, disability rights advocate, and lecturer.

Ildefonso was a Mexican migrant who was born deaf and lived in Southern California for much of his life. He did not obtain any structured language until twenty-seven years of age, when Susan Schaller volunteered as a sign language interpreter in an adult school.

Before language, Helen and Ildefonso attempted to communicate using crude signs and gestures, acting out what they wanted. In her autobiography, *The Story of My Life*, Helen writes that a pull on someone meant "come," and a push meant "go." When she wanted bread, she would imitate cutting bread and buttering it. If she wanted her mother to make ice cream, she made her crude sign for using the freezer and shivered.

In her book, *A Man Without Words* (first published in 1995), Susan Schaller explains that when she tried to sign or connect with Ildefonso, he copied her movements. And when Susan stopped, Ildefonso stopped. In one lesson, Susan taught Ildefonso the sign for "tree." She also drew a tree on a piece of paper. Ildefonso mimicked her and nothing else. He didn't grasp what she was trying to convey.

Imagine playing Pictionary, but you only have the image of the card in your mind. You don't know what it's called; you don't know any words; you don't know how to read, and you can't understand what people are saying. How do you play? How do you win? The only way this seems possible is if the participant brings you exactly what you want. How likely is that to occur?

Susan wrote, "I tried once more to explain without language that language existed, to explain without names that everything had a name. I failed, and his face showed that he knew he had let me down. We were only inches apart, but we might as well have been from different planets; it seemed impossible to meet."

Have you ever forgotten the name of an item you want someone to bring you? It's on the tip of your tongue, and it's driving you crazy because it's not a hard name; you simply blanked. Now imagine you don't know the name of that thing at all. Imagine you don't know each item has its own distinct name. As much as we pride ourselves in our imaginative abilities, that experience is not compatible with our experience of reality.

When Helen and Ildefonso learned that names existed, it transformed their experience of reality entirely. Their lives were never the same again. This is not dramatic; it defies imagination. When Helen learned that W-A-T-E-R was the name of that cool something that was flowing over her hand, she stated that the "living word awakened my soul, gave it light, hope, joy, set it free." She learned everything had a name, and each name gave birth to a new thought. As author Justin Cronin writes, "There is power in a name. It is through names that we bring all things into this world, and when they leave, it is names we carry with us, so they are never truly gone." That same day, Helen learned many words, including *mother*, *father*, *sister*, *teacher*. The awe in this experience cannot be overstated.

Susan spent days working on *cat* with Ildefonso. The letters C-A-T, *cat* the sign, mimicking petting a cat, *cat* on the board. When he realized *cat* was the name of the animal, his entire experience changed. "Suddenly he sat up, straight and rigid, his head back, and his chin pointing forward. The whites of his eyes expanded as if in terror...my body and arms froze in mime-and-sign dance that I had played over and over for an eternity."

When Ildefonso got that C-A-T meant something, his "face opened in excitement as he slowly pondered this revelation... slowly at first, then hungrily, he took in everything as though he had never seen anything before...he slapped both hands flat on the table and looked up at me, demanding a response. 'Table' I signed. He slapped his book, 'Book,' I replied." With his face in tears, Susan signed for him the names of the door, clock, chair.

Susan wrote about Ildefonso, "He had entered the universe of humanity, discovering the communion of minds. He now knew he and a cat and the table all had names...he could see the prison where he had existed alone, shut out of the human race for twenty-seven years." Helen wrote she learned the name of every object she touched, and the more she learned, the more "joyous and confident grew my sense of kingship with the rest of the world."

Helen and Ildefonso's first revelation was the discovery of names. After this first step, their language acquisition progressed at different rates. More importantly, there was no going back to the way they were before.

Many years after they first met, Susan spent time with Ildefonso and his brother Mario, who was also deaf. Mario never acquired sign language and still conversed in crude signs, mimes, and gestures. Ildefonso wanted to show Susan how they communicated in that way, but he couldn't. "He turned to me and apologized, explaining he could no longer gesture and mime with his brother the way he used to. He knew too much American Sign Language (ASL). Language had changed him and his thinking."

The point is this: language is as critical to the human experience as it is distinct from it. You and I can never imagine being without language. Ildefonso, who began to acquire ASL when he was twenty-seven years old, couldn't go back to communicating in a gestural way, even with his own brother. Helen said before language it felt like invisible hands were holding her and she couldn't free herself. Ildefonso simply commented to Susan, "You-you knew me before." Both Helen and Ildefonso have a distinct understanding of what life was before language acquisition and how life transformed after language acquisition. The yearning to communicate ultimately found its path forward through the help of teachers.

Language transformed our species. We saw how language allowed our species to flourish and thrive to become the only human beings on this planet. We also see that when we don't have language, we are trapped. People who have injuries that affect their language capabilities also express their frustration with their inability to communicate as they once could. A human being without language does not experience life like a person who has language. A person missing limbs or a person paralyzed can order a meal at a restaurant, tell jokes, express love, tell stories of the ones they grieve. How they function in the world is different, but we experience a whole human being. I invite you to try this on as you continue through this book: your experience with language is different than the phenomenon of language, and by separating them you will begin to create a space to master language.

As seen with Helen and Ildefonso, this mastery flows effortlessly in the direction of language acquisition once that door is opened. This movement serves our species well in continuing the normal course of our lives. Your normal use of language has allowed you to pick up and read this book. Yet you chose this book for more than the normal use of language. Mastery is what we seek. To master language, we must explore the amazing ways we use it and identify the ways it molds and shapes our world to our benefit and our detriment.

USING LANGUAGE TO CREATE MYTHS

As far as we know, only *Homo sapiens* can talk about entire kinds of entities they have not seen, touched, or smelled. As Yuval lays out, legends, gods, and religions emerged after the cognitive revolution. "This ability to speak about fictions is the most unique feature of sapiens language."

Two Catholics who have never met have the shared religious myth of Jesus Christ dying for our sins. Two US soldiers who have met for the first time may risk their lives to save one another because they believe myths of duty, honor, nationalism, or the American flag. Two lawyers who have never met can combine efforts because they believe in the legal myths of law and order. Yuval brilliantly points out that people easily understand that "primitive" people cement their social order by believing in ghosts and spirits and gather during a full moon to dance around a campfire but take for granted that our modern institutions function on the exact same basis. Look at business entities. A corporation is a legal fiction, existing only on paper as a legal person who you will never meet nor ever could. It's a far stranger tale than that of a guardian animal spirit.

This all revolves around telling stories and getting people to believe them. And when the stories succeed and people believe them, it gives our species immense power, and we can organize millions of people to cooperate and move toward common goals, like creating churches, states, and legal systems. These are called fictions, social constructs, or imagined realities.

Yuval explains, "Imagined reality is something that everyone believes in, and as long as this communal belief persists, the imagined reality exerts force in the world." We also have the objective reality of things we can see and touch. These two realities are the basis of our very existence. What's more, imagined reality often becomes more real for us, and the ability for myths to shift makes them even more powerful. We see these as cultural evolutions, which are much faster than genetic evolutions. Almost overnight, the French people went from believing the king was anointed by the divine to believing in the power of the people.

Our shared myths are the cornerstone of organizing millions of people not present in any other species of animals. Insects may have the numbers, but the way they organize is much more rigid. Yuval discusses how chimpanzees can organize in groups up to 150, but any more and the social structure breaks down. One hundred people can also be organized by the personal relationships among the members, but even military groups of hundreds, thousands, and tens of thousands need shared myths to remain organized: the myths of hierarchy, order, respect, and purpose.

Rather than "imagined reality," we will refer to "internal reality." We do this because, as we discuss, our ability to imagine reality is not limited to shared myths. We impose myths on others as if they believe them. And we interact with them based on those myths. Much of the time, this is the origin of conflicts, disagreements, offenses, and the like. We do this so subtly that we don't know the difference between our internal reality and their internal reality. In this vein, we treat our internal reality as external reality. Instead of "objective reality," we will use "external reality."

USING LANGUAGE TO GOSSIP

Another principle use of language is gossiping—namely talking about other humans. Yuval says gossip comes so naturally to us that it is like language developed for this very purpose. It is often said that human beings are social creatures; however, this is more than an observation. Language enables us to engage in complex discussions, analysis, and decisions about other people: their thoughts, motivations, desires, etc. "Does he like me back?" "Did you hear what he said about her?" "How can she like a guy like that?" "I heard he doesn't really like her." "He wants me to fail." All these are messages regarding interpersonal relationships. This is obvious as it is fundamental to our use of language. What's more, we don't need other people to gossip. We gossip to ourselves about others. We can conduct a whole analysis and arrive at a decision about others without their or anyone else's participation. The decisions are typically judgments.

We humans are amazing at making judgments. We make

judgments about brand-new people we just met simply from the context of our encounter: at a coffee shop (stranger), work gathering (cannot be fully candid), family gathering (be careful what you say). These contextual judgments are quickly followed up by personal judgments: their skin color, clothing, hairstyle, posture, eye contact, height, weight, smile, tone of voice, mannerisms, vocabulary, etc. This is equally easy with people who we already know. We "know" how our siblings are. We "know" how our parents are. We "know" how our friends are. We "know" how they'll react to news, to conflict, to sadness, to joy. We "know" this because we have made judgments about them. However, when we focus on what we know (judgments) about people, we are not engaging with them; we are engaging with our judgments. Even if you correctly guess their response word for word, you are not engaging with them; your guess was created wholly in your mind. The reward for your accuracy is that you rely more and more on your judgments about them, which means you rely less and less on your experiences with them.

You may already see the unique approach this book takes to language. If you had no knowledge of evolutionary biology or life without language, you may have read this chapter with an open mind and a willingness to learn. If this is the case, I invite you to continue reading this book with that perspective. If you had judgments that arose regarding this chapter, I get it. As we already discussed, we humans are well equipped to make judgments. You may instinctively critique, judge, or dismiss some statements or exercises. Judgments serve us well to avoid danger, pick partners, and choose our favorite foods. However when engaging with new material or engaging with material newly, our judgments can interfere with experiencing the material.

With this in mind, I welcome you to notice your judgments as they arise and put them aside. I encourage you to read this book and remain open to anything that comes up for you as it comes up. When you encounter resistance to a sentence, paragraph, or chapter, I request you acknowledge it, put it aside, and continue. When something connects with you and you want to explore it further, I request you acknowledge it, earmark it, and continue the book. Experiencing the completeness of the book will set you up to address anything that comes up for you.

Of course, however you arrive at this material is your choice. There is no right way or wrong way; there is only the way you choose. Let's begin.

CHAPTER 2

Step 1: Receiving the Message

The first step in any communication is receiving the message. Let's consider the following messages.

- I'm happy.
- Your dog barks loudly.
- He doesn't like you.
- He and I had a great time yesterday.
- We don't have enough food for everyone.
- She won't return your text.
- I'm not feeling well today.

These phrases are simple, and you may hear them on any day. As of right now, they exist only on this page. Here are other communications you may recognize.

"We shall fight on the beaches, we shall fight on the landing grounds, we shall fight in the fields and in the streets, we shall fight in the hills; we shall never surrender."

—Winston Churchill

"Give me liberty or give me death."

—Patrick Henry

"So, first of all, let me assert my firm belief that the only thing we have to fear is fear itself—nameless, unreasoning, unjustified terror which paralyzes needed efforts to cover retreat into advance."

—Franklin D Roosevelt

"Yesterday, December 7, 1941—a date which will live in infamy—the United States of America was suddenly and deliberately attacked by naval and air forces of the Empire of Japan."

—Franklin D Roosevelt

The historical phrases and the simple communications above have a few things in common. First, they are complete communications. Clearly, the historical phrases are part of much larger speeches; however, that does not make these communications incomplete. The whole speech is a different communication. Parts of those historical phrases are recognizable without the full sentence. "The only thing we have to fear is fear itself." You may know a US president said it; you may even know it was FDR, but you don't know the entire speech. The words of Winston Churchill and Patrick Henry are equally identifiable and don't require more context to recognize.

Another thing they have in common is that we have no personal context for these communications. The simple communications are modern statements but only words on a page right now. Without identifying the speaker, through making judgements about them and the context, they are just messages. Likewise, at the time of this writing, it is very unlikely that any living person heard the speeches contemporaneously and has memories associated with them.

So these simple and historical communications are complete, and we have no personal context for them. These two points seem obvious. Here's the kicker: these two points are true for all communications. The words stated are a complete communication. The utterance of them is all that is needed for the message to exist in this world. The old philosophical adage of "if a tree falls in the woods and no one is around to hear it, does it make a sound?" is answered with a resounding yes.

Why is this important? Well, have you ever uttered the phrase, "I need some space?" We have an innate understanding that "space" interrupts what will occur or allows for something to occur. "Space" allows us to analyze the message and get a handle on everything that comes up for us. This is usually done in order to control our reactions to the message. However, we will take this same mechanism a step further and use it to separate receiving the message itself, Step 1, and processing the message, Step 2. The conflation of receiving the message and processing the message does us no favors.

DISTANCING YOURSELF FROM MESSAGES

Let's say Person A utters sounds, which are waves. These sound waves travel from Person A to Person B at 343 meters per second. At the end of their journey, as it relates to us, the sound hits our ears. The sound enters the ear canal and causes the eardrum to vibrate. The vibrations then travel through three bones in the middle ear, which amplify the vibrations and send them to the cochlea in the inner ear. The cochlea is a snail-shaped structure filled with fluid, and the vibrations cause the fluid to move, which bends thousands of hairlike cells. These cells convert the vibrations into electrical impulses that travel along the auditory nerve to the brain, which interprets the signals.

Communication has begun! The message, however simple, innocent, hurtful, or off color, has left Person A and made its journey to you, Person B. People dismiss this obvious fact outright. Every communication starts this way, so we naturally don't sense it or appreciate it. We typically start our communication experience with our analysis or our response. We have no sense that this step is part of communication, or even important. What value does this add?

Have you ever been told, "Don't take that personally"? You may respond, "How can I not? Did you hear what they said?" In our day-to-day experience, our first engagement with communication starts with the meaning of what Person A said. It does not start with what Person A said. It starts with the meaning of what Person A said. "Meaning" is not Step 1. The communication itself is Step 1. "Meaning" is something you determine. That is not a Step 1 experience. We are breaking down the experience of communication into manageable steps.

Have you ever tried to kick a ball without moving your leg? How about throwing a baseball without winding up your arm? While these may be accomplished comically, they are disasters as far as quality of the movement and mastery of the craft. Our goal is mastery of language.

The first step in communication has nothing to do with you, what you think it means, or what you want to say in response. With this logic, the communication cannot be personal to you because it doesn't matter what was said. Even if the statement "Hey you, (first name) (last name). I hate your guts." Step 1 is the communication itself.

You can immediately do this for anything anyone says to you. Insert this step into every communication you receive. You will see a distance created from Person A's message to your reaction to it. To really get a sense of Step 1 as distinct and real, you may even go over the mechanical parts of Step 1 that enable the message to reach you. Do this for messages you give yourself also. Remember, all communications are simply language. It does not matter the origin of the message; it is all language. If you tell yourself, "You're stupid for making that mistake," stop and just get the message that comes to mind. Don't make judgments about the message: "That's true," "No I didn't," "I shouldn't say that about myself," "I know I can do better," etc. Don't engage the message (that comes later). Right now, simply pause and get the communication. That's it. In pausing, you will sense the distance between the message and what comes next.

PRACTICING CREATING DISTANCE

"I have a dream that my four little children will one day live in a nation where they will not be judged by the color of their skin, but by the content of their character. I have a dream! I have a dream that one day, down in Alabama, with its vicious racists, with its governor having his lips dripping with the words of 'interposition' and 'nullification' one day right down in Alabama little black boys and black girls will be able to join hands with little white boys and white girls as sisters and brothers."

—Martin Luther King Jr.

Was reading those words the same for you as reading FDR's words? Or Churchill's words? For most of the readers from the United States, I would imagine the answer is no. Why is that? Because you connect the historical words to other things in your life. You create context with other memories, judgments, decisions, and experiences in the realm of race relations. Whether you fall on the side of the dreams being realized or the side of "we have made little progress," those are judgments which come from you, not the communication. You can no easier separate your thoughts and comments on the speech than pulling apart a piece of thread lengthwise.

Why does it take significant effort to stop at the end of the communication and not go into the other comments, feelings, and judgments that come up? First, stopping at Step 1 is unnatural for us. Language as a separate existence is foreign to us. Our minds make hundreds of decisions that we are unaware of. The decisions we are aware of are only possible because of the mind's ability to complete tasks on its own. One of those tasks is to process language. The mind does a lot of work we are not conscious of but reap the benefits of.

When your eyes are open, you can't stop yourself from seeing. Input enters, and processing of the items, surroundings, and people is done instantaneously. You make no conscious effort at all. To add to this wondrous mechanism, you unconsciously decipher what you see, and you can name the items or answer questions about them. I have a headset on my desk, and I know it's a headset. I can identify other headsets that may look different but are still headsets. Going back further, images that enter our eyes are inverted so the brain turns them the right way up when it processes the information. We use this information to maneuver in our external world every moment. Getting up from our chair, leaning against a wall, reaching for the door handle, hugging your kids—all this is made easy with visual input and processing.

Language is the same. It is innate, and much is done without our conscious effort. Our conscious thoughts are only the tip of the iceberg. Language processing allows us to maneuver in and manipulate our environment, from reading a sign, communicating danger to our companion, expressing wants and needs, etc. Our ability to use language to communicate to ourselves and to others is only a small portion of our language processing ability.

We don't need to think of the name of a person or object before talking about it. We do not need to relearn every morning when we wake up that everything we see has a name. We do not experience the wonder of our relationship with our physical world. When we go outside and feel the warm sun on our skin, we are not experiencing the sun rays traveling 186,000 miles per second to reach our body after a trip of eight minutes and twenty seconds. What we experience is warmth. Likewise, when the barista says good morning, we are not experiencing the wonder of hearing a person speak, understanding the person speak, and responding in the same language of a stranger. We hear a nice greeting. Our minds do tremendous work, leaving us able to interact with the world.

But if we want to effectively utilize language, we must first dismantle it. I took salsa dance lessons for a number of months, and many students wanted to do spins quickly but couldn't maintain their balance. They often said they could do them fast but struggled when they slowed down. Our instructor taught us that control is necessary, and you must learn to control going slow or you will not be able to move fast with control. To master dancing, you must slow down and break down the movements. To master language, we must slow down and break down language. "Dancing is life" correlates well with "Language is life."

The importance of Step 1, receiving, cannot be overstated. Someone's communication has nothing to do with you. It's physically impossible for a communication to be fundamentally about you because their communication is language, composed of words that travel along waves and into your mind where you process and understand them.

You can experience this. Not only can you but you must. Why must you? Because the communication you've had all your life does not experience this distinction. And it is the best place to start when mastering language. Start at the beginning. In language, the beginning is not about you. It's about the message.

As you experience identifying the message and stopping at Step 1, you may experience a change in your relationship with the message. The communication seems further away. It is not personal. It isn't attacking you, trying to get you, annoying you, etc. It simply exists. You will notice your response to the communication is separate from the communication. Your feelings, opinions, and judgments are not part of the message. You will sense a space opening up between the communication and your processing of it. This is a real experience. The experience of this space is critical in mastering language. You can only intentionally process messages if you can see that processing is a separate experience from receiving. This newly revealed space is where we can process messages with new tools and identify what comes up when we engage the messages.

EXERCISE 1

The most powerful messages to apply this technique are with messages you tell yourself. The adage, "You're your own worst enemy" is not just folk insight; it is a very real experience many people have. Self-talk can be empowering or debilitating. Our task is to exercise the muscles of Step 1. And the beautiful thing about exercising this muscle is you can do it anytime with any message. You can do this intentionally or naturally as a thought occurs for you.

For example, express a positive comment about yourself. Say it out loud. "I am a nice person." "I look lovely today." "I am a good friend." You may notice after reading one of these you have an automatic response. Or you may feel the urge to say something more but then decide not to. This is good. Notice how you automatically generate a response to the positive statements. Notice and sit with the real experience that you have something you already want to say in response to them. Maybe you agree with the statements and approve of them. Maybe you want to explain them away, such as, "I'm not really that nice of a person," "I do look good today but lovely is going too far," or "I try to be a good friend." Any and all reactions to the original message are responses.

You may have noticed that within these positive messages and the corresponding responses, you participated in all three steps of this methodology. If you didn't notice, then know that you did. We will delve into the following steps later. For now, I want you to experience that the message stands alone and requires nothing else to be a message. You will flow from message receiving, processing, and responding so smoothly you'll be amazed at how adept you are at this. Language acquisition and expression are easy for us; control is not.

For now, continue to identify the message. Pry apart the original message and any reaction to it. Just identify the message and stop. If you continue to Step 2 and Step 3, try again. Say the message again and stop. Repeat this three times with the same message. Continue until you can do this successfully three times in a row with the same message. Do this throughout the day. When you get up for a water break or to use the restroom, do it again. Use the same message or a new one. The key is to practice. Just get the message.

I also recommend doing this with negative messages. "I am a mean person." "I look terrible today." "I'm a bad friend." There is nothing special about these particular phrases. I chose them as examples because they are short and reflective. Pick any message you like, but keep it simple. You are using language for the first time in this way. Don't overcomplicate it with large statements, complex ideas, or outlandish messages. You are developing a muscle you likely have never used. Start slow and simple.

There is nothing special about positive or negative messages either. You may be catching on that even calling the messages "positive" or "negative" is not part of Step 1. If you are, very good. If not, that is okay. I use these types of messages for two reasons. First, you have an instinctual reaction to the messages because when reading them, you already identify them as positive or negative. You must notice this instinct and practice interrupting it. Second, life is filled with positive and negative thoughts, and when you use these at the outset, it will help you refine the muscle to do Step 1 no matter the message that is received.

You may feel like you're tripping over your own two feet. Great. I cannot stress enough how unnatural this is. You have spent your entire life using language one way only. And you will struggle doing this. Fantastic. Keep practicing. Identifying the message separate from anything else is an invaluable tool.

Next, apply this to messages you receive from others. This may be easier after reading the next chapter, but there is no harm in trying. You are playing with language in a way you never have. Congratulations You are on your way to mastery.

CHAPTER 3

Step 2: Processing and Context

In *The Language Instinct*, a phenomenal book I read during my personal development journey, Steven Pinker describes how we, human beings, are wired to learn and use language. We assume the sounds we hear are in a language we can identify, and our assumptions are often rewarded as we can understand the sounds we hear as relating to a language we understand. We group the sounds into words and then further into phrases. The individual phrases are understood, and their relationships to each other are decided, which then helps us understand the entire sentence. Not only that, but we do this repeatedly with several sentences, understanding that the same subject is referred to without the name being repeated after the first sentence. We may even mishear a word but can derive the intent of the sentence from the context of the other words with remarkable accuracy. In that same vein, if we are told what was said was different than what we heard, when we hear the correct words, we can correct our listening to the words so that if the same phrase is repeated again, we hear it with the correct words, not the incorrect ones. We have different words with different constructions depending on whether the sentence involves the past, present, or future; whether the sentence refers to a person, two people, or multiple people; whether they are known people or high-status people.

All this is automatic. We do not actively try to understand every single word we hear or every sentence we receive. We do not access vocabulary like opening a computer file. Our minds do this profoundly well and automatically. It doesn't end with vocabulary either. Grammar is largely universal throughout all the world's languages, with sentence structure changing depending on whether the language is a subject-oriented language or a context-oriented language. Our ability to keep the object or subject in context as we receive more information and understand it is truly phenomenal. We do not choose to understand the words we put attention to. We do this instinctually.

If Step 1 of receiving messages is completely unacknowledged, Step 2 is largely corrupted. We cannot repeatedly distance ourselves from all the judgments we automatically make when receiving thoughts and communications; we have to eventually acknowledge how past experiences, present decisions, and future fears affect those messages. That means delineating between what exists because of you and what exists separate from you.

This context is crucial to engaging with the outside world. Our ancient ancestors learned not to eat those poisonous berries because they saw someone else eat them and die, or they were taught not to eat them, and because they abided by that rule, you appeared on this planet thousands of generations later. Context is so crucial in our everyday existence that it is automatic. When your alarm goes off in the morning on a weekday, you don't have to decide your next step. Weekday means workday. Even if you need to confirm if you have work that day, you don't consciously decide on the individual steps. You get up from the bed and walk from the bed to the bathroom, all without deciding to move your legs, deciding how many steps to take, or identifying that you must put on clothing because not doing so would be problematic.

Can you bake a cake with all the ingredients dumped in the bowl at the same time? Of course not. I'm no baker, but even I know that everything has its order and timing. Likewise, you've likely spent your entire life not differentiating between your internal and external realities, but to attain mastery, you must begin to do this.

UNDERSTANDING INTERNAL AND EXTERNAL REALITIES

Let us go back to one of the simple communications at the beginning of the last chapter. "Your dog barks loudly" is a complete communication. You may know this, but I really want you to feel this in your bones.

Let's do a mental exercise. Close your eyes and imagine you are in a professional sports stadium, and in the middle of the field is you and one other person. You do not have a dog. You and he are six feet apart, and he tells you, "Your dog barks loudly." Now let's say you are in the same location but standing 300 feet apart. He calls you on your cell phone, and in the exact same tone, he says, "Your dog barks loudly." Next, he is standing right next to your left eye, head almost touching your head, and he says, "Your dog barks loudly." All three scenarios are the same communication; what changed was the context.

To complete Step 1, what we can say for sure at this point is the message "Your dog barks loudly" does not belong to you. It is not yours. You do not own it, and you are not required to acknowledge it for it to exist. Here it exists three times, all the same communication.

Now we may begin with Step 2. Context, by definition, is the circumstances that form the setting for something else. The settings in our work can be understood as realities. As we introduced before, in the world of language, we have internal realities and external realities.

Let us start with the external reality. The external realities of the scenarios above are (1) standing six feet apart, (2) standing 300 feet apart, and (3) standing inches away. In all three, you are standing in the middle of the field in a professional sports stadium with no dog. Pretty straightforward. Let us note that in this example, there is no internal reality before the communication. For our purpose, you are simply standing there. You don't know the person and make no judgments about them (we will return to this shortly).

In a different example, let's say you are walking your dog down the street, your external reality, and you hear the words, "Your dog barks loudly." You may look at your dog in wonderment and see if he's barking. You may think, *Did he bark recently? If he barked, did he bark loudly?* All these things would have happened in the external reality, so you can try to remember if or when they happened. If your dog has barked in the last twenty seconds, you can assume the communication likely has to do with your external reality of your dog having barked. This person must have been around your dog in the last twenty seconds and heard him bark.

Again, in the above example, there is no internal reality before the communication. There were no decisions made about the person who spoke. You don't notice every single person who is around you when you walk your dog, so it is fair to assume this person didn't draw your attention before the communication. In this example, the communication came first, and then the reality was developed.

The distinction between internal and external reality can be messy and confusing, especially in the beginning. Why is this? For one, our default as human beings is to believe what we decided. And we make decisions about reality, both internal and external, unconsciously and consciously. We don't naturally distinguish between internal and external because we don't need to. Humanity has survived as long as it has doing exactly what it does. We interact with our decisions as if they are true, whether they are about internal or external reality. Doing this allows us to play the game of life. Playing the game of life is what we do every day, but what we seek is mastery.

The short definition is this: external reality identifies information about the world. Internal reality creates information about the world.

Let us add some internal context to the example of the person who said, "Your dog barks loudly." After you investigate the external reality of your dog having barked or not, you automatically make a decision about the person. If your dog didn't bark, then you may think, *That person is crazy*. If your dog did bark, you may think, *They should mind their own business*, or *The bark wasn't that loud*, or *So what? He's a dog*.

Each comment is an internal reality. Let's break these down. If your dog didn't bark and you decide "this person is crazy," you have made a judgment on the person for the communication they generated. You could end with the decision on the external reality that your dog did not bark, but we don't naturally do that. Why is that? Because our experience with communication is that it requires a response. In most cases, the decision we come to is some type of judgment. "He's crazy" is a judgment about the communicator because their comment/message doesn't match external reality. If your dog barked and your thought is, *They should mind their own business*, then your judgment is, "What my dog does or doesn't do doesn't concern you." "The bark wasn't that loud" is a judgment of the loudness of our dog's bark and how it wasn't loud enough to cause a disruption or warrant a comment. And because it wasn't a disruption, this communication is unreasonable or wrong. "So what? He's a dog" is a judgment that a bark is a natural behavior for a dog and is not disruptive to anyone, as it is natural, so this communication is unreasonable or wrong.

You may have come up with your own judgments with regard to the example, but one thing is clear: any decision you made *after* the communication and *after* checking your external reality is a creation of your internal reality.

RECOGNIZING OUR INTERNAL REALITIES

What does it matter if a reality is external or internal? Well, our realities are created in language. As we have seen with Helen and Ildefonso, language literally alters our experience of life. With external realities we have something outside of ourselves (external) to which we are putting language. If you identify a four-legged canine as a wolf, your experience with the canine is very different than if you identify that same canine as a husky. We can look at those external features to decide on the external reality.

With internal reality, there are no external points to refer to or decide. If we had those, it would be a creation about external reality. Assuming your memory works normally, you have many memories in your head. Memories of things you have done and had done to you. Memories of decisions you made and conclusions you came to about the motivations and goals of others (judgments). These are internal realities. They exist solely in your head. You may say, "No, this thing really happened." If I ask you to recount what happened, it is very likely your recounting is made up of both internal and external realities. Why is this? Because you likely have never had the tools to distinguish between the two.

More importantly, the internal reality that exists is built on other internal realities that exist. Stories that go back for years are evidence of your current internal reality. When writing this section, my sister came to me with something she is dealing with. My sister has an eighteen-year-old son, and she is terrified of acting the way our mother did when my sister was eighteen years old. Her ex-husband also tells my sister, "Don't act like your mother," which "makes" my sister stop and doubt every comment and decision she makes. I talked with my sister about what she is afraid of, and she told me her story about what happened when she was eighteen. The story included what happened, what my mom was thinking, why my mom did what she did, and how my mom made my sister feel. And my sister's fear is built on the fear of all that repeating. It was truly a great talk with my sister.

Even now, you can see the way my sister was telling her story was full of external and internal realities. External reality is what happened. My mother said things to my sister. Internal reality is what my mom was thinking, why my mom did what she did, and how my mom made her feel. My mother didn't communicate her thoughts or reasons to my sister. My mother went radio silent after their last talk. My sister decided my mom's thinking and reasoning. The phrase "they made me feel ____" is common among people. How you feel is largely an internal reality. No one can make you feel a certain way. People can do external things. People can say, "I'm breaking up with you," or "I hate you," or stop talking to you. Those words can be said, and those actions can be taken or not taken. That is the external reality. How those words impact you is the internal reality. And they do have an impact. My sister's current fear is based on the internal reality she created when she was eighteen, over twenty years ago.

Let's say Person A is a coworker/friend-enemy. You don't really get along with Person A, but you run in the same circles. You see them often and are never happy to see them. They often dismiss what you say, and their compliments are backhanded insults that annoy you at the least and infuriate you at worst. Some would say you have history with this person. You have dealt with them enough to have decided you don't like them. You may not share this with anyone. You may have other words you tell yourself about them. All this is there even before they tell you, "You look nice today. What a change in pace for you." All this is your internal reality. It is what is present for you before the message is ever received.

This is not a foreign idea and not limited to our communication with others. You look at your phone to see your mother calling you, and you have a "knee-jerk" reaction, as we call it. "What does she want?" "Not now," "Yay" (mothers would prefer this be our reaction), "I'll call her later," "Now is not a good time," "I don't want to get stuck on the phone." These reactions are not based on the incoming call from your mother. That is just a phone call from your mother. Your reaction is based on your history with your mother, your experience in the past. These are all things you tell yourself before your mom even has a chance to utter a word. You may have felt targeted and have years of evidence to prove these reactions are just, necessary, and completely understandable. That's not the point of this example, so put those justifications and self-righteousness aside. This is not about judgment. This is to show the vastness of internal realities.

When you are asked to give a presentation to high-level corporate officers in your firm, the style of presentation, word choice, and outfit are all affected by context. Your turn at Pictionary on game night with your friends doesn't require your best suit or your mastery of verbiage to ensure you come off as knowledgeable and professional. The basic acts are the same, while the contexts are widely different.

When looking at our examples of the different types of presentations, it is obvious how the two realities differ. The context of the events are drastically different, and our participation in them is also drastically different. No one would see an issue with these. The reason these are so obvious is that when the external realities are clear, the internal realities are much easier to identify and create.

The first two examples in this chapter are less clear because the mix of internal and external realities is incredibly hard to identify. The internal discussion about the phone call from your mother occurs entirely in your mind. That is pretty clear. But your reasons for those thoughts were justified because of past experiences. Let's say you talked to your mom yesterday for one hour about something unimportant to you. You use, "I just spoke to her yesterday. What could she want now?" as an excuse not to answer. If this is our capstone (the top block on a pyramid), what building blocks are we using to support this? The external reality that you talked with her for one hour. You talked about _____. That is the external reality of what happened. What is the internal reality? "The conversation took an hour." "It wasn't about anything important." "It took time away from doing other things." "I would have preferred to do _____ instead of talking to my mom." What does her phone call right now have to do with a phone call from yesterday? Well, in this example, nothing. You have no idea why she's calling you now. It could be about the same thing, some good news, some bad news, or a funny cat video she saw. The point is you have no idea what the phone call is about, but you have lots of evidence to lean on that it isn't something you want to deal with at the moment.

Answering or not answering are choices to make, but when you're going over all the reasons to make a choice or are exacerbated by the annoyance of the call, you aren't simply choosing; you are justifying, reacting, and analyzing. But you aren't analyzing the content of the call, rather the occurrence of the call. Let's say you answer the call, and your mom just tells you she loves you and is looking forward to your next visit. What if she tells you she has been diagnosed with cancer? What if she wants to tell you about a show she is watching (my mom's favorite pastime right now)? The point is, while you wrestle (internally) with the call occurring, you don't deal with the actual external reality of the incoming call. Answer or don't answer, and move on. Wouldn't it be nice to be that decisive and productive? Internal realities are complex and subtle, but the more we identify them, the less influence they have over us.

Internal realities are extremely tricky because we can build upon them as if they are external realities. For us, they are true and decisive, and they cannot be changed. We build on internal realities as if we created them intentionally. It is very likely the majority of your internal realities were not created intentionally. My sister doesn't want to fear being like my mother, but she does it anyway. Would you intentionally create a fear that brings up more fear and anxiety? Of course not.

If our internal realities are not created intentionally, then how were they created? They were created automatically. Why? Because we create them using language, and just as Helen and Ildefonso wanted to put names to everything around them, we naturally want to put names and meaning to everything around us. As a species that uses language in a way no other species around us does, we yearn and automatically use language to assign meaning to reality. And we generally have no distinction between external and internal reality. Because we use language for both, we give deference to our language, with no concern of internal and external realities. In essence, we believe everything we say about a reality simply because we said it. We need no convincing. In this way, language has us; we don't have language. And because this distinction doesn't affect our basic human functions, it persists. This is why I often repeat, "We want mastery." We aim for more than continuing life as we know it.

DISMANTLING INTERNAL REALITY PYRAMIDS

As I discussed in the introduction, after my father's death, I managed his business with the incessant thought, *I will not be my father.* As a child, my external reality was that my father, almost daily, came home very late. Sometimes he was at the office working. Sometimes he was with his social groups. But I often fell asleep without seeing him. When he picked me up from school, I was often the last student because he was delayed with work.

My internal reality was that my father didn't love me. He

preferred to have people praise him and use him rather than spend time with me. He was selfish, prideful, and self-centered. His business and his groups were more important than me. And I would never be like him. And because he *was* the business, I didn't want it because it would mean I would need to be like him to have it.

How do you think those ten years of running my father's business went when coming from a place of "I don't want to be my father"? It was hard. Harder than it needed to be. This is where the pyramid comes in. This was the capstone of my internal reality with my dad's business. Everything that followed underneath had to support the capstone of "I will not be my father." Why is that? Because that was my focus.

Have you ever closed your eyes and tried walking in a straight line? Try it, and you will naturally drift to your dominant side. This is natural. It is also natural that what you focus on becomes the capstone of your internal reality. Everything that supports your capstone exists to reinforce it. And your previous decisions on internal reality become the building blocks of a new internal reality pyramid.

"My dad was self-centered" was the capstone of a pyramid I built about my dad. I had evidence to support this. His staying at work late and participating in various groups where he spent time and money were evidence he was selfish and self-centered. And I used this pyramid as a building block for my new pyramid of "I don't want to be my dad." The block of my dad being "selfish and self-centered" served as a sturdy foundation for my new pyramid. And I used the pyramid of "I don't want to be my dad" as a building block for the new pyramid of "running his business." Can you see how that made the process harder than it needed to be?

There is no limit to the amount of times we reuse pyramids. In fact, the more we reuse a pyramid/building block, the sturdier it becomes, and the more widespread we use it. Our continual reuse of it reinforces the "truth" for us. And it is *only* its reuse that reinforces its importance, its value, its truth. And its reuse is largely automatic.

You may ask yourself, *What does not wanting to be your dad have to do with running his business?* If you say nothing, then you are correct. It has nothing to do with it. After ten years, I was able to separate the two, so I no longer had that block in my "running his business" pyramid. I was freed up because I wasn't fighting myself. Have you ever had a position, opinion, feeling, or judgment that made something more difficult? Maybe it negatively affects your job or your relationship with a specific person. What disparaging comments do you tell yourself? "I can't do something." "It's too hard." "I'm too old." "I don't have the money." "I'll never find love." "I always pick the wrong one." "Why does this happen to me?" What building blocks do you use under this capstone?

Pyramids are a great image because they stand the test of time. Pyramids such as the Great Pyramid of Giza, Chichen Itza, Machu Picchu are known for their stability and longevity. The strength of the building blocks makes this possible. And if we do not address our pyramids and our building blocks, they will stand the test of time for whatever capstone we have there. "I'll never find love" will be a monument to your life. "My father never loved me" will be a building block for "I can never trust men." "I'll never make anything of myself" will be supported by all the things you did not succeed at. Pyramids often used adhesives like mortar and cement to layer blocks on top of each other. Our pyramids are made up of internal and external realities. By separating the internal and external realities of each pyramid, we disassemble each block—the once-formidable "truth" of our reality. Decisions layered on decisions, based on previous decisions, which are a mixture of internal reality and external reality, and we no longer know what is what. The more pyramids we dismantle, the more we see those building blocks are our creation. How so? Because external reality identifies information about the world, and internal reality creates information about the world. Pyramids are not naturally occurring. We have created them, which means we can choose how to respond to them. We can either allow them to be a part of our experience, or we can put them aside and dismantle them.

Internal realities are created by us automatically, so when we separate them from the external realities, we must choose what to do with them next. I recommend you put them aside and let them go. Why? Because you did not create them. Putting effort and attention into understanding your automatically created internal realities gives credence to them. By engaging them you are stating they have value. We understand this in our human experience already. The notion of "letting go of the past" best mimics this experience; however, the basis is quite different. We start with identifying the external reality. Then we identify the internal reality. The internal reality is all our creation: an automatic, unintentional creation. Letting go of the automatic, unintentional creation sets you free to create.

I encourage you to practice this first. You have lived your life giving power to these internal realities. I encourage you to intentionally remove their power and let them go. There is no risk in doing this. Why do I say that? If you successfully let them go whenever they arise, then you continuously experience how they are not what you want to create. In this experience, you don't need to wrestle with them. In this experience, they are more of a comfort/crutch than something you really identify with. If you struggle with putting them aside, then this is a signal there is a pyramid there. In that case, you have revealed there is another space where you can apply this work.

Again, the reemergence of the automatic internal realities will occur, especially in the beginning. This is not a problem. Don't create judgments about their reemergence. You are human, and your mind will do what it does best: automatically create meaning. Your experience with the emergence of these automatic realities is what matters. If you can put them aside, they will emerge less and less. If you struggle with putting them aside, then apply the work. It is likely the automatic internal reality that comes up is actually composed of internal and external realities. Why is that? If you are clear that all internal reality is your creation, then it has no inherent value. Your struggle with it is likely based on the "truth" you put on a piece of external reality that is mixed with your internal reality.

I acknowledge you delving into the intricacies of your internal and external realities. That is where you will discover what really is in your space, what really is in your way, what you really decided in the past, what you really fear, and what you really want to create in your life.

EXERCISE 2

Let's go back to the self-messages we used in the exercise at the end of the previous chapter. The positive messages are: "I am a nice person," "I look lovely today," and "I am a good friend." Let's now focus on those automatic responses that come up. There are many paths for these auto-responses to take. In regard to "I am a nice person," what comes up for you may be "I'm a decent person," or "I try to be," or "I don't think I'm particularly nice." You may pick one to work with that resonates with you. An automatic response that resonates with me is, "I'm no nicer than the average person."

There is no getting this auto-response "right." Any response will do. I encourage you to pick one that resonates with you. Why is this important? Because what resonates with us reveals some of the pyramids we use as building blocks for our life. Since we use language for everything, we have pyramids for everything. Some of these pyramids are quite limiting. Others may empower us, until they don't. The point is, by using responses that resonate with us, we are developing the muscle to identify and work with pyramids.

"I'm no nicer than the average person" is my auto-response for this exercise. What does this response reveal about me? What is the context I am creating with my response? How is this different from the message? The message "I am a nice person" needs nothing for me to receive it. So why add context? For the purpose of this exercise, let's put aside the fact that you created this message. The origin of the message doesn't matter at the moment, only your response. Also, this auto response will likely occur if someone else told you the message, "You are a nice person." Why is that? Because your context is a response to the message.

We have said this repeatedly, but I want to make this abundantly clear. You did not intentionally create your response. It only exists as a response to the message. It is a reflex, a twitch, an instinctual creation you had no power over. Why is that? Because the message is connected with decisions you have already made about yourself and about the world. These decisions are not top of mind but are strong pyramids that you are not even aware exist.

"I'm no nicer than the average person" means I have a

standard of how nice the average person is. I have made a judgment about my personal niceness compared to the niceness of the average person. Being "no nicer" than the average person is another way of saying "I'm average." "You are a nice person" is largely meant to be a compliment, so let's identify this as a positive message. Am I experiencing the message with my response? Do I experience "I am a nice person" with my response? Absolutely not. The context I created is only tangentially related to my niceness. It's related in the sense that I am applying my context to the niceness and corrupting the message.

You may say, "Well, it's your own message, so that's okay."

What if your best friend told you, "You are a nice person." What if a stranger you helped with a random act of kindness told you, "You are a nice person." What if a bystander saw you perform that random act of kindness and told you, "You are a nice person." Would you resist the temptation to apply your own context to the message? Of course not. In this context, my "normal" response would be to downplay their message. I would say something along the lines of, "Oh, it was nothing." Letting in compliments and acknowledgments has typically been hard for me. And when they happen, I have to stop myself from adding my own context. Why do I do this? Because I want to honor the message. I want to hear what they are saying. And if I put my own judgment in the way of their message and my getting it, I cannot do that.

If I really take a look at the pyramid of "I'm no nicer than the average person," what is revealed is far more personal than simply a standard I apply. Why must I apply any standard at all? Even if there was a universal standard, which is highly debatable as common courtesy is largely cultural, why would I judge myself as average? If this connects with you, then I offer you this: I resist positive messages. My instinct is to downplay, ignore, explain away, etc. And that is because one of my building blocks about myself that repeatedly shows up is "I don't deserve that positive message."

In the same way, a person who receives a negative message may be triggered and become defensive. If someone gives you a negative message, the first step is just to receive the message. But we don't naturally stop there. When we get defensive or confrontational, it is because we apply our context in front of their message. "Who are you to judge me?" "You don't know me." "I don't care what you think." These are all automatic responses to a negative message. And these auto-responses reveal something about you in regard to interacting with negative messages.

Auto-responses are a normal use of language. As you learn these tools and get used to applying them in every message, it is because you have chosen to do so. I stress this because judging those who don't have these tools is simply building another pyramid and another context you are applying. Your choice to learn, apply, and practice these tools gives you the opportunity to get people's messages like you never have before. And they will experience you getting their message like they never had before.

I use the term "put in front of" the message very intentionally. Your application of a context that you autogenerated is a corruption of the message. It is as simple as that. To put your context "on the message" makes it sound like putting on a jacket or coat. When we put something on something, sometimes we can convince ourselves it looks better, looks right, or fits well. This is essentially conflating Step 1 and Step 2. You will continue to do this. How do I know? Because you are human, and this is how we naturally use language.

Mastery does not stop this. Mastery allows you to identify that you are doing it before it has an impact on you, and choose a different path.

I want you to experience "put in front of" as if you are in a storm—snowstorm, windstorm, rainstorm, sandstorm; it doesn't matter. A storm only interferes with vision. In no scenario does a storm make vision clearer. Likewise, there is no way your context makes the message clearer. It only interferes with, corrupts, degenerates, and dishonors the message. This is not to say that all messages are clear and easy to understand. Of course not. But if you desire clarity on a message, then go to the source—the messenger. Trying to figure out the message on your own, in your own head, does not reveal the message. You simply are creating a new one, which you incorrectly believe is the one the messenger said.

For this exercise, identify the contexts that you are putting in front of the message. Applying this with negative and positive self-messages will not be as difficult as applying this to messages from others. Applying it to other messages will take practice and honesty with ourselves. Why is this? Because you will want to naturally identify parts of your context as part of the message. "That is what they meant," you will lament. "I know this because I know them," you will explain. If you justify a context and you can't point to the message as the explanation, then it is likely you are relying on your years of experience and knowledge to arrive at the context. And remember, you have done this your whole life, so it feels right and natural. It is normal, and you did not choose normal. You chose mastery. So keep practicing. And good for you for doing the work. We don't always like to exercise, but we get results when we do.

As you see, we built on Exercise 1 from the previous chapter. This is easy to do because we are breaking down a process that happens in seconds. Like watching a high-speed video of a shark breaching water, we can see the individual movements only by slowing down the speed of the video. Likewise, here, we are slowing down language processing so we can identify the parts. That being said, it is okay to practice Exercise 1 only, or Exercise 2 only, or both in sequence. There is no right or wrong way to practice. I simply caution you, again, that if you are adding judgments during your practice, you are building another pyramid, which you do not want to do.

CHAPTER 4

Step 3: Respond

Reviewing some archetypes may be helpful to see the automatic mechanisms you used to generate a response to a message. These are illustrative and not conclusive. Your automatic response may be a combination of these examples.

The Gunslinger is one who responds like a challenger drawing a gun in a gunfight. The communication, whether it's a response or a generated message, comes quickly. Being first is key. Why is it important to these communicators? I have no idea. You may know someone who speaks first, then clarifies, elaborates, changes their mind, and changes their mind again, all within a short period of time. Their processing occurs in real time and could give you whiplash.

The Pinball is one who is scatterbrained. They cannot make a decision. They are either paralyzed by fear or overwhelmed with things to consider. It's like they are all over the place. A decision is rarely made, or if made, it is never satisfactory to them because they were never clear on what they wanted or what outcome they wanted. Picking a restaurant or firing an employee can be too much for this communicator.

The Whirlpool is someone who follows a possibility to its most extreme and terrifying conclusion. Like a snowball getting bigger as it rolls down a hill, they follow the possible outcome of one decision by a possible outcome of another decision, so far and so forth, until the ultimate conclusion is reached. The response to the conclusion is so real they treat it as an external reality.

The Great Communicator seems flawless in their delivery of their message. They may listen intently and respond enthusiastically, and overall they are impressive. They can be annoyingly in command of their environment and themselves. Do you know someone who fits this description? Your reaction to such a person may reveal more about your internal realities than about the Great Communicator.

The point is that "how we know ourselves to be" is a creation based on the totality of our lives. You may have experienced these as constraints that cannot be changed. Like your natural hair color, it is simply the color it is. You can change it temporarily, but the true color will always come through eventually. As you see, this is not true.

During Exercise 2, you may have seen some ways you typically act or react. My "I don't deserve that positive message" reappears over and over again whenever I perceive a message as positive or complimentary to me. This is my archetype of how I respond to positive messages about me. What recurring self messages do you deal with? What do you repeatedly tell yourself that comes up in a variety of situations and messages? This repeated message you may have struggled with throughout your life. "I don't stand up for myself." "I shut down when confronted." "I hate fighting." "I say things to hurt people even though I know I shouldn't." See what message comes up repeatedly in your life. This may be an archetype you can choose to address. This may be a pyramid that is consistently in your way, but it's now your opportunity to choose to dismantle it.

DISMANTLING THE PYRAMID OF YOU

How can the tried-and-true pyramid of "I know myself" be wrong about you? Do the work. Every message can be dismantled with this system and should be. If you know yourself as a shy person, it doesn't mean you are a shy person. You having thirty years of evidence of being a shy person doesn't mean you are a shy person. Why does none of this matter? Ildefonso knew how his life was until he began learning language at twenty-seven years old. The experience of language changed him forever. Nothing about what he *knew* before he learned language mattered at that point. He learned and created a new existence.

What you *know* about yourself was all created in language through a combination of internal and external realities created by you. External realities of being turned down by your crush in high school when you asked them out occurred, and you created the internal reality of being "unlikable," "unlovable," "ugly," "not worth it." If they laughed when you asked, the internal reality you created was, "I'm a joke," or "No one will take me seriously." If they were apologetic, the internal reality you created was, "They are patronizing me," or "They don't really care about my feelings," or "They think I'm a loser." Even a polite "No, thank you. I'm not interested" could be met with the created reality of "Who are you to turn me down?" or "I didn't really want to date you anyway," or "You're a bitch," or "You're so stuck up."

Now that you are practicing understanding and utilizing

language, you can dismantle your pyramids and remove the blocks that sustain them. When you dismantle these "truths," you are left with the undeniable truth that there is no *you* aside from what you create. You can see the external reality events for what they are: just events. Nothing more. Events that happened. Anything you add to those events is a creation of internal reality. You can now let the internal realities go.

Every human being has events, moments, and circumstances that we feel are critical to our identity. Holding my father's hand as he passed away was one such moment for me. Coming home twenty minutes after he passed away, collapsing in the bathroom and crying out all the pain in my body was another. You may have similar moments of loss. You may have moments of feeling victimized, abused, harmed. You may have experienced truly horrific events, or joy you cannot recreate and seek out helplessly. Applying the work to these moments is particularly powerful and difficult. It is difficult not because the language we use for these is unique; it's difficult because we have used these pyramids over and over again, and they are part of our "identity." Personal development coaches will tell you that you must become comfortable with being uncomfortable. There is no more uncomfortable place to be than dismantling a pyramid/building block that you see as part of you. I acknowledge you for taking that on.

UTILIZING TILES, NOT PYRAMIDS

We do not want to create pyramids. We, as a people, do not require pyramids of decisions to run our lives, nor should we seek to create them. It is not to say we should avoid building decisions up on decisions; that would largely be unworkable. The great examples of human achievement are built upon one decision after another. Personal development coaches and their predecessors will tell you that successful people have failed more times than unsuccessful people have tried. Avoiding being decisive or judgmental is not the mastery we are seeking. Being free of all the building blocks that hold us back or get in our way is the mastery we want.

Step 3, Respond, is more aptly understood as Create. In a response, the communication is creating the message in Step 1. You may have noticed that people construct their pyramids in reverse. We have the capstone, and then we pick the blocks we put underneath to support the capstone. The capstone is the communication. Once we have it, we find support for the communication. This clearly isn't a good strategy because we aren't creating a communication; we're justifying it (we will address this later).

The pyramid model doesn't work for mastery because it's too inflexible. Instead of building blocks and capstones, I use something more easily manipulated and arranged. Post-it Notes are a much more flexible tool. Post-it Notes are lightweight and easy to move around. I prefer to envision these as dominos or mahjong tiles to feel the weight of them and slide them effortlessly around a table. Why these small, easily maneuvered items? Because they are easy to create with and reflect the malleability of language. They also serve as a reminder that we have language; language doesn't have us. The mastery of language is not overly complex and doesn't require special tools; however, it does require practice.

Let's apply these to my previous pyramid of "I don't want to run my dad's business." In the pyramid, I had all the bad things about him and made them mean something about the business. "I will be a workaholic," "I won't have time for my family," "My work has to be the most important thing." Even the capstone referred to my "dad's business," when it was mine. So what can I do? First, I write all these building blocks onto separate Post-it Notes. For example, "I don't want to be my father," "I hate how his business was organized," "I don't want to be a workaholic." I will no longer experience them as solid blocks but merely ideas/messages. Capture as many of them from your pyramid as possible onto Post-it Notes or tiles.

Second, I write what comes up for me when thinking about my dad's business; what I actually want to do. "Run it well," "Make it different," "Make it how I want it," "Honor my father with it," "Have a balance between life and work." This could be a form of word vomiting or free writing. Get every sentence written down on a separate Post-it Note or tile, and review them. If a new one pops up, then make a new tile. When you feel like everything is there, look for what will be your lead tile or header tile.

In my example, I will try my old capstone of "I don't want to run my dad's business." You can ask yourself, "Is this what I want as the lead tile (the tile by which all other tiles support)? Is this statement what I want to create? Is this something I want to do (namely, 'I don't want to run my dad's business')? Is this what I want to focus on? Do I want 'I don't want to run my dad's business' to be on my mind when I'm actually running the business?" I think it's clear the answer is no. This is not an empowering communication. It is not inspiring. It is not motivating. It is detrimental.

Notice we are simply picking the tile and seeing if it represents what we want. We are not searching for evidence to support the tile. We are not justifying the tile. We are choosing the tile. We are not weighing the pros or cons of the tile, the barriers in our way of creating the tile, the cost of it, the time commitment, the people we have to interact with, etc. The only analysis is, "Is this what I want to create?" In this example, does it reflect the business I want to run? Clearly it does not. Running away from my dad's business is not running toward making it my own business. Since I decided it does not reflect what I want, then I move on to the other tiles. I'm not judging the tiles either. "How could I have written that on a tile?" is a judgment on your tiles. Don't do it. It doesn't help anything at the moment. (That may be another pyramid you want to tackle later on, but stay on task.) You may look at all the tiles and realize what you really want isn't there, so you add more. That is completely fine. You are creating, and there is no right or wrong way to do it.

I ultimately landed on "I can make the business my own and honor my father at the same time." That became my lead tile. That was my header tile. With the pyramid removed and my tile chosen, everything in my world changed. I could see that I could choose my dad's business as my own, transform it so it worked for me and my family. What became possible suddenly changed. Once you pick a lead tile, it's time to create new tiles to support that main tile. Things will emerge that you didn't have room for before. I could be at peace with "I love my dad" and "I'm changing the business." I could think of services to offer or discontinue without being restrained by my "dad's" business. I was confident I would no longer do things the way my dad had while looking forward to the new. Back then I didn't have the concept of tiles, but in practice, this is what I did. Each of these new quotes could have been a tile. They fed the lead tile of "I can make the business my own and honor my father while doing it." I created what I wanted because I chose to. You will face difficulties in doing this. You have spent your entire life building pyramids and using those pyramids to build new pyramids. This automatic function will not disappear. The more you do the work, the faster and easier you can remove pyramids and create new tiles. This will be imperfect, and that is okay.

Creation is not justification. They may seem the same, but they are different. My creation of "making his business my own" had nothing to do with the practicality, hurdles, cost, time, stress, effort, etc. Creating had nothing to do with "I must," "I should," "I need to," "My family needs me to be the patriarch," "It's necessary," "If I don't, who will?" etc. Choosing for choosing's sake—that is creation. The other things were things I had to deal with. The circumstances I had to face did not disappear, nor were they magically resolved. But I didn't deal with them because I had to; I dealt with them because I chose to.

Let's go back to the phone call from your mother. We discussed all the reasons and justification for your internal reality. The response/creation to that incoming call would be to answer it or not answer it. Nothing else is required. If you see an incoming call from your mom and decide you won't answer now, then don't answer, and move along. You have chosen to not answer. If you choose to answer the call, then you are listening to the communication from your mother, instead of the communication *you* created about the call from your mother. Do you see how answering or not answering did not require any of the reasons and explanations you could have juggled?

Imagine you are the driver of a car. The road you are on is your trajectory at that moment. This is a normal experience of our life. Being on the move, doing whatever you are doing, picking roads to go down. For example, you could be heading to your office at work. As you walk inside your office building, you see that annoying coworker heading straight toward you. The pyramid of "I don't like this person" emerges from the ground directly in the path of the road as you knew it. The road you are on no longer exists, and instead, the road changes to go around the pyramid. This is seamless because things occur all the time that change your path. Instead of just thinking about what you have for lunch, you now have the pyramid of "I don't like this person" to deal with. Whatever your destination was, it now includes a new obstruction/destination—namely, annoyance with this coworker.

The occurrence of something unexpected and having to deal with it is easy for us to understand. A flat tire on the way to work, the barista getting your order wrong, forgetting your lunch at home are all unexpected occurrences. These may "ruin your day," and there you have a pyramid of "My day is ruined." The pyramid has now changed your road, and you experience more of "My day is ruined" because that pyramid will persist if you insist "my day is ruined." Throughout your day, as more things go "wrong," you will add blocks that support your capstone, "My day is ruined."

You may even try to convince yourself your day isn't ruined. You try to look at the positive things that are occurring or you are looking forward to. This, however, isn't dealing with the pyramid; it is building another pyramid of "My day isn't ruined" and providing evidence to support that. This is essentially fighting yourself, working on trying to prove one is correct. This isn't creation. The new pyramid exists only as a response to the "My day is ruined" pyramid. Creation will be if you go to your "My day is ruined" pyramid and dismantle it. What happened? My coffee order was wrong, and now I have a drink that I did not order. That's the external reality. What did I say it meant? My day was ruined. My internal reality. Just because I said, "My day is ruined," does that make it true? No, it doesn't. I am not saying you cannot be upset about the error, but the impact it has on you is your choice. You can dismantle the "My day is ruined" pyramid by looking at the building blocks and separating external and internal realities. With the building blocks dismantled, you see that the capstone "My day is ruined" has no support, so you can choose to put it aside. Just because you said, "My day is ruined," doesn't make it true.

COMMUNICATING FREELY

Have you ever told your spouse, sibling, or child to do something, and they didn't say anything in response. Perhaps a side-eye acknowledgment of your request is made but they never said they would do it? Does that drive you crazy? What if they communicate and their communication doesn't warrant a response, or your response is likely to be an explosion (because you haven't mastered language yet), so you keep your mouth shut. Not all communication requires a response, but all communicators want a response.

Now, sometimes what they want is to aggravate or hurt you. I am not advocating acceptance of the communication as truth or of having any value. In cases where there is nothing you want to say or feel you should say, I use the following for Step 3. "I got it." "I got it" does not mean agreement, acceptance, or disapproval. It simply means you received the message. Try this on someone who knows you to be reactive and watch confusion wash over their face.

Imagine responding to someone with no pyramids corrupting your communication. In other words, imagine driving with no pyramids in your way directing where you end up. When you see that annoying coworker, the pyramid of "I don't like this person" has already colored whatever they say. The only destination is "annoyance" because of your pyramid. Now imagine you see that person, and you stop yourself after your first complaint about them. You see your pyramids rising as you drive and know where they will take you. So you stop and put the pyramids aside (so you can dismantle them later), and now you're left with open grassland. Is your predetermined destination "annoyance"? Of course not. With no roads leading the way, you can just be ready to receive the message.

The work we do in Step 2 sets us up with an open space to create our communication with no pyramids present. As you formulate your communication, pyramids will pop up, and when they do, you will dismantle them or put them aside until you can. Responding from nothing creates new conversations, which will create new relationships, which will change your world. Applying these steps, you will see how many judgments you have made about people. Once you identify the judgments (pyramids), you can put them aside. Like a game of freeze tag, once you see it, you can identify it, and it can no longer participate in your experience. The more you identify, the more pyramids you put aside, and you open your space to create your communication freely. With your space open, you can choose for choosing's sake.

When you have no internal reality associated with an external reality, what is the power of the external reality? It has none. I held my father's hand as he took his last breath and promised him I would take care of everything. Now, when I look back at that event, that external reality, I am not burdened by my promise. I told my father that so he could pass away knowing he didn't have to worry, but I lost sight of that for many years as I wrestled with the burden I felt. I now look back at that day, and I connect with the love I have for my father—the gratitude for having him in my life for as long as I did.

In this way, you are the architect of your life. You are responsible for the internal realities you create. Put aside or dismantle each pyramid as it comes up. Discover how you intertwined internal and external realities your entire life. Identify the external reality; identify the internal reality. More likely than not, your previous internal realities were made automatically, building on previous automatically created internal realities. Once you decide you no longer want that capstone as part of your reality, create something new, a lead tile, and shape your world.

EXERCISE 3

Now we deal with the pyramids that pop up when you create the messages we have dealt with in this exercise. As a reminder, the messages are "I am a nice person," "I look lovely today," "I am a good friend," "I am a mean person," "I look terrible today," "I'm a bad friend." When these messages appear for you organically or automatically, we have a tendency to engage with them automatically. I want you to take a moment and remember, acknowledge, and experience that this is not necessary. Just because you have interacted with them automatically for all your life, that has no bearing on what you choose to do now. While these messages seem pretty harmless, the muscle we are developing is to interrupt the automaticity of our language creation. As humans, we are all too familiar with the process of spiraling, or continuing down a path of unstoppable message creation. This occurs because we don't have the tools to stop it; this is what we are developing.

This tool applies to all messages. Spiraling can occur with all types of messages. Whether you focus on your faults, your greatness, your triumphs, your failures, etc., there is no topic where we are incapable of spiraling. Do not take this as to halt you from exploring or experiencing these topics. However, there is a difference between exploration and spiraling. Your experience with the topics will largely inform you of which you are participating in. And if spiraling occurs, it is because there are pyramids that have emerged. If this happens, great. You now have the opportunity to address them.

Create "I am a nice person." Say it out loud. Once you set aside your resistance, just experience the creation. This will feel like your world has expanded and is meaningful, while at the same time it will feel like something is missing. What's missing is what is automatically created in language. You won't miss it, but you will instinctively feel the gap this area once occupied. It will be uncomfortable. Congratulations. You are experiencing and practicing being comfortable with feeling uncomfortable. At the same time, the expansiveness of your experience may surprise or scare you. When you experience the ultimate power in creating your world, your experience of what you are capable of creating feels limitless.

This space of creation is key to allowing yourself to experience the power of creation. We are so adept at putting stuff in the way of our experience that when we remove it, what is left can almost be playful. Creation is intentional, but it need not "feel" a certain way. By stopping the automaticity, you will feel differently about how you interact with your life. Things will emerge in areas you never considered. Creation will occur in ways you never imagined before.

CHAPTER 5

The Act of Creation

My ex-wife and I have two children, ages seven and six at the time of this writing. Both of our sons are autistic. I eat dinner with our children at my ex's home on most weekdays, and I help our children with their homework. Their mother and I talk about our days, things that came up, how our families are, etc. My oldest has a series of questions he asks me and wants me to ask him, and we are sure to cover these. After dinner, I help clear and clean the table while their mother gives our youngest a shower. I usually do homework with the oldest. After he finishes, he takes a shower. If both boys shower at the same time, then I take one and help dry and dress them. They take several medications, so I prepare them for their consumption. During this time, their mother is also busy putting things away, cleaning dishes, cleaning up after the kids, helping her mother, etc. We've developed a fine working relationship during the week.

On the weekends, I typically see my children on Saturday evening, and we often go out to eat or run errands. On Sundays, if we aren't doing an activity, we run errands together. I emphasize I do this with their mother and our kids together. Their mother and I converse like normal adults. We laugh. We get passionate. We disagree. We switch between topics. It's a dynamic we chose.

For those of you who do not find this situation weird, I commend you. For those who do find it weird, I get it. For years, my mother agreed with you. My ex-mother-in-law and some other friends and family did too. As I am typically a private person, I had few others who gave me input in my situation. My ex faced a lot of disbelief. We would go together to the kids' events, parent meetings, IEP meetings, etc., and my ex would explain to other parents that we were going through a divorce, and they didn't believe it. They were surprised. As the divorce took longer than anticipated, some of her friends voiced skepticism if we were really getting divorced. Her mother often said, "You guys get along. You shouldn't get divorced."

Why is this weird to so many people? Well, in my society, and likely yours, this isn't "normal." There is a shared idea/myth/understanding of how divorced parents should act. These common myths are shared by a majority of the members of a society. Societal members didn't choose these myths intentionally. They didn't create the internal reality of how family dynamics "should" work. Like much of language, these were all learned automatically in the course of living our lives. We have countless pyramids made from countless other pyramids/building blocks that we did not intentionally create. As we discussed earlier in this book, most we are not even conscious of. And myths change. The myths of racial superiority that justified slavery are no longer controlling my society. The myth of the divine rights of kings and queens was dismantled by the innate rights of human beings. Shared myths change over time and can be measured in generations.

CHANGING YOUR MYTHS

You can change your myths whenever you want. You can create new internal realities whenever you choose. Your new internal realities, when seen and experienced by others, will change others' myths. You will create new common myths. After a few years of my family experiencing my internal reality with my ex by including her in our activities, creating new external realities, they created their own internal realities where co-parenting looked like what I had created and not what they had in their mind previously. My ex-brother-in-law was largely not around for many years, but after seeing my dynamic with my ex, he was slowly given the opportunity to reintegrate with the family. He became more present for all of us. In that way, he was more present for his kids, and he helped me and my mother when we needed it. Our family as we knew it previously changed entirely. The myth that we created of "what family is" changed for my family, and our lives are richer for it.

The type of father I wanted to be, the type of co-parent I wanted to be, was my own myth that clashed with that of my mother for a time. Also, when my ex and I first separated, we were contentious, as many partners are. The family I now have was not accidental. It took practice—making mistakes, trying again, and continuously practicing. It also took something for me to be honest with myself and allow myself to be surprised by the actions and decisions of others. The pyramid of identity is not limited to "you." You also have pyramids for "them." "Them" being anyone and everyone else in this world—even people you have never met nor ever will. Identities you have created for others because you "know" them or "know enough."

You have an area of your life where you feel restrained, limited, held back, unexcited, burdened by, or unfulfilled. This could be personal relationships, career, health, confidence, etc. Pick one, and start working. At the beginning, you will need to commit to doing the work in one area at a time. You will work up to doing this work in all areas of life, but starting with intentional practice in one area is a great first step. You will feel like you're getting it wrong, not doing it right, won't ever get it, etc. Apply the work to these thoughts. Every thought/message is an opportunity to apply this work. Why? Because we use language for all of it. If it is not abundantly clear yet, this personal development work is entirely personal. Meaning it all begins and ends with you. The wondrous thing is that through your work, the world changes. Eventually, whenever you feel uncomfortable, uneasy, or bothered, you will know it is time to intentionally apply this work to whatever is coming up for you.

What new myth will you create that will change your life?

COMMITTING TO PRACTICE

There are days I wake up in the morning and tell myself, "I hate this." It may be one of those mornings I am wholly unexcited. There may be something specific that day I can blame for waking up in the morning with this perspective, but this can also occur without any identified reason. "I hate this" can come in different flavors. "This is going to suck." "I'm not excited about today." "Ugh." "I just want to stay in bed." "I don't want to do this." These are only a few varieties. While writing this book, I had such a day where the first thing I told myself in the morning was "I hate this." The "this" I was referring to had no specific identity. It just was. And because it was not and could not be identified, "this" became everything. "This" was walking to the bathroom, getting ready for work, thinking about my to-do list today. With no boundaries, "this" was everything.

You are very familiar with this. When your concerned partner asks you if you're okay and you exasperatedly say, "I'm irritated," and they ask you why, you snap back, "I don't know." Often "I don't know" is a placeholder for "You should know," or "I'm not going to tell you." But let's assume you really don't know. Or at least you can't pin it down. There are so many reasons to be irritated, who can choose? What's the typical human response? Is it acknowledging that our current experience of "I'm irritated" is a capstone, and we could find every irritation in our lives to justify this capstone, essentially making everything we do difficult; so then we realize the best thing to do is to stop using that capstone and use a different one? You wish. "I'm irritated" means your unidentified, boundaryless irritation will be applied to everyone, and everything you encounter and think. Or worse, it will be targeted to specific people or things, which you have not decided irritate you but will be the recipient of your irritation.

Why does our general irritation color everything around us? You know by now we have used it as a capstone. With "I'm irritated" as a capstone, we can easily list all the reasons that build and support this pyramid. The famous Henry Ford quote fits nicely here: "Whether you think you can, or you think you can't, you're right." "I'm irritated" and "I can't" are capstones we created. We constantly talk to ourselves, and because our voice and thoughts are always present in our lives, we often think they hold more truth than other communications. Nothing is special about the words we say to ourselves. They are not more true, more honest, more real, or more accurate. They are simply communications. When we remove the aura of authenticity of our internal communications, it's almost comical that we accept capstones as if they are true.

Let's go back to my morning lead tile of "I hate this." My

solution was to change the lead tile to "I'm okay." Easy, right? Of course not. Just because I say, "I'm okay," doesn't mean I believe it. It doesn't make it true. But "I hate this" wasn't a true statement either. It was a tile. Nothing more. How do I know that? The simple answer is I created "I hate this." That message came from me. As I created it entirely, I can switch it out with another. I can create something else. If all communication is created, we are the authors of it all. The capstone "I hate this" reemerged several times for me. Each time I switched it with the tile "I'm okay." Four or five of these switches, and I could now focus on my new lead tile and create supporting tiles. Again, not because it was true but because I created it and chose it.

You can choose any communication to apply this work to. What you must do is apply it repeatedly. The more you apply it, the more your proficiency will improve. In the beginning, this will seem taxing, counterproductive, unnatural, annoying, etc. Good. It should take something for you to do this. Language as a phenomenon serves a purpose, but it does not serve *our* purpose. Humans use language to maneuver our lives daily and continue on our "normal." Our purpose is to create the lives we want in a world we want. We want to master language and create with it. If we master it, then we can do that with ease.

Have you ever experienced a quietness in your head and heart where things seemed very clear? Some can achieve this through meditation. Others can name a few moments in life where everything came together and they seemed like perfect moments. The first thing you will notice after doing this work is the interruption of the automatic language generation.

Like a car braking hard at a stoplight, you will feel an abrupt change in momentum. This will feel odd, and you may not know how to describe it. It won't necessarily be a good or bad feeling, but it will simply feel different. The act of putting aside or dismantling your pyramid is this braking. Like trying on a new pair of shoes, you must walk in this a bit to see how it really feels. If you continue to do this work, something new will emerge. After you feel the stop, you will see space in front of the stop. An open space. A space where you can create. This space will be like a flicker at first. Why is that? Because your mind isn't used to this, so it will try to automatically put things back in. It will try to keep you moving again along a road you did not choose. But keep doing the work.

The open space in front of you will become more real. I can feel it in my gut. You may feel it in your head or your heart. You can give a name to this space, but I caution you against that. Some may call it hope or possibility, but why label it? Feel it, and relate to it like Helen Keller and Ildefonso when they first discovered language. This space requires no language to experience. You can identify it, feel it, experience it, and then create from it without labeling it. This space is real.

The more you stop, put aside a pyramid, and dismantle it, the more the space will appear. And you will sense that you can create in this space. Instead of pyramids, you use tiles, so there is nothing in your way. Previously we discussed you being the driver of the car. That is how most people feel in their lives, moving in a world they simply deal with but have no control over. But this is not true. You are the driver, the car, the road, and the space itself. You experience life through language, and you generate the language, whether intentionally or automatically. By removing the automaticity of language (the pyramids) you can then create intentionally (with tiles). Once the pyramids disappear, you are left with an open space, a grassland where you can drive anywhere. The boundaries and limitations you put on yourself no longer exist.

Continuing the driving analogy, as you begin to create in this space and travel this open space, you will see new things pop up. New landmarks you may want to visit. Structures you want to create. Bridges you want to connect. You will see opportunities as little flickers of light on the horizon. You will be able to choose where you go and what you create along the way.

This book emerged in this way. I knew there was something else I wanted to do aside from beginning to work in special education law. I started working on a language coaching program. As I began working on it, I knew I wanted to really get into the details, so I started writing. But as I was writing, more questions emerged, so I did more research. With more research, I realized my writing was becoming more expansive, so I decided to write this book. As you can see, there were numerous points when I could have stopped just because of what was coming up for my writing. "I can't." "It's not working." "This is taking too much time." "No one will read it." "Does this work?" "Who am I to write this book?" These were all things that popped up for me. But my lead tile was "This is going to make a difference." And it has for me. And it will for you.

The experience of "knowing there was something else I wanted to do" emerged in a space of exploration. When you identify what's in your way and put it aside, you are left to explore what is possible. What's more, when you are free to explore what's possible, you start being drawn forward into it. The best image I can use to illustrate this comes from science fiction. A tractor beam works by attracting an object to it. That "something else" was my tractor beam. I didn't know what it was, how I would get there, or what it would do, but I knew it was there. You may experience this as being "inexplicably drawn to" someone or something. As you experience being drawn to something, your proficiency in this work grows, and your application of this work becomes more natural. You experience doing the work without doing all the steps. This will come naturally with mastery and ultimately reveal a fundamental truth.

THE TRUTH ABOUT PYRAMIDS

I rarely use pyramids anymore. This may come as a shock, but keep reading. Let's take a high-rise view of pyramids. What are our pyramids made of? Language, of course. And what word have I used repeatedly in this book when discussing engaging with language? The word I have used, and its sibling varieties, is choice. Choosing. Our true power as humans is our ability to choose language. I'll say it again, as it bears repeating. Our true power as humans is our ability to choose language. So true mastery of language is the muscle to choose it. Choose the language you want to engage with.

So why don't I use pyramids anymore? Because I chose not to engage with my pyramids. Not only that, but I know I created the pyramid. It doesn't matter if it was created automatically by me; it was still created by me. Why is this important? Because I can choose to dissolve it without dismantling it piece by piece. You will resist this experience until you can let it go entirely. Nothing created in language is permanent. This is obvious as it is difficult to experience. For those of you who go to "But they said this," or "How could I forgive them for saying that?" this is still true for you. What you are holding onto is what those words meant to you (your internal reality), not the actual message (external reality) that occurred sometime in the past. I will say it again: nothing in language is permanent. That is my experience with language now. Nothing I said twenty years ago, or what I said every day, is permanent. What does this have to do with my pyramids?

Pyramids are not permanent either. The tool set offered here is for you to develop, address, and experience this. It is a fundamental truth that we must experience to get. I can tell you about a beautiful sunset, but if you experience it yourself, my words are worthless. Like many adages, "Experience is the best teacher" is true. Pyramids are made up entirely of language. Knowing this and experiencing it are different. When I identify a capstone, the first thing I do is to choose if I want to engage with this capstone or not. If I don't want to engage with it, I choose not to. I see it dissolve like cotton candy in water. It just melts away. I'm not putting it aside for later. Putting it aside for later for you to work through is a great skill I still use when needed, but I experience that all thoughts and messages are simply air, mist, clouds, cotton candy, which I can easily do away with if I choose. And I have that power, and I have experienced the power because of the muscle I have trained with the exercises I have done.

So I don't deal with every pyramid that emerges because I know I made it, and I can just as easily unmake it. I do this without engaging with it. You have the experience of thoughts, comments, and automatic responses that are not in line with what you are up to. Not in line with what is important to you. This is almost instinctual. This is also not explaining, listing, or analyzing. Trust your gut. Also notice that if you say you put it aside and then keep engaging with it, you have not put it aside and need to do the full exercise as we have discussed in this book. This is an advanced process. Like the spins in dancing, once you master the pieces, putting it together feels and looks seamless. When these pyramids occur, when that capstone emerges, I choose not to engage with it, and I move along. It's quite simple. It's simple, though it is not easy.

If you can't, won't, or choose not to put it aside immediately upon identifying the capstone, ask yourself this question: "Is this a message I want to interact with? Do I want to engage with this message?" This question will help you create the space between Step 1 and Step 2. It is a way to be present to the power you have in the advanced process. If at this point you decide, "No, I don't want to engage this message," then put it aside or watch it dissolve, and continue along your way. If you "can't" put it aside, or you struggle with it, don't force it. Forcing it only creates a new pyramid. Do the work in this book.

There is nothing wrong with doing the work in this book compared to the advanced process presented in this section. Some tools work better for some than others. There is no judgment from me about which you use, nor should there be any judgment from you. Any judgment from you is (say it with me) you creating another pyramid. That is the one thing you don't want to do. And if you do create or identify another pyramid, great! Now you can choose what to do with that one.

YOU CAN PUT LIPSTICK ON A PYRAMID, BUT IT'S STILL A PYRAMID

Pyramids will never go away permanently. So the good news is you don't ever have to worry about destroying all your pyramids because you never will. Why is this? As we've discussed, many pyramids are automatically created. Our mind uses many automatic processes and assumptions that benefit us greatly. Vision, body movement, and sweating (temperature control), to name a few. Our language processing and creation is only one of these automatic processes. And we don't want to eliminate all of them because that would be detrimental to our human organism and the experience of our lives. Pyramids being impossible to eliminate should be comforting but could be annoying to others. Be at peace that they will always exist.

However, much like bacterial infections, the more we treat them, the more they change. In the case of pyramids, they become better at camouflaging. We can't see them right away. If we're practiced enough, we can notice that something is off, but it can elude us. Much like the alien from the Predator movies, we know it's there, but we can't see it. We sense it. This is my primary experience with pyramids now. My experience of life is clouded and off when something I can't identify or see is in my path. You have experienced this too. Something is off or doesn't feel right; you're irritated, nervous, stressed, etc. You can't name it (because if you could, you could deal with it), but you know something is off.

At this level, what works best for me is giving myself space to explore what's there. Just let the cloudiness exist. I don't dwell on it, and I don't try to figure it out (if I were ready to figure it out, I would have already). I let it exist because if I create that "I need to figure this out now," I am creating a pyramid about the experience (which we want to avoid doing). Being with the feeling that something is "off" or "wrong" is not the same thing as creating "This is off and wrong, and I need to stop it."

Much like the ineffable experiences of happiness, joy, and grief, the experience of disconnectedness is its own experience. It does not need language, and the application of language does not always help. After my father passed away, my mother and I went to group grief counseling. One thing that really stuck with me was the description of grief as waves in the ocean. Grief, as an experience, is not something you can avoid. Much like walking into the ocean, you can only lean into it to make headway in your path forward. The experience of disconnectedness is a sign for me. It's a sign that something is disconnected. So I lean into it periodically to see if what is there becomes revealed to me. I don't avoid using language to figure this out, though I don't stress if it doesn't help immediately.

And just like grief, the process of leaning into it at the right times makes your progress faster than if you resist it. To continue the water analogy, when you are caught in a riptide, you swim parallel to the shore, not directly against the current. Allowing yourself to experience the space of disconnectedness will allow you to discover what is actually there for you. And I have found what is there for me is often a repeating message I tell myself, just harder to locate in the clouds.

In this way, doing the work continuously, exercising consistently, and giving yourself grace when it doesn't go well right away will reveal far more to you than you ever imagined.

LIMITLESS APPLICATIONS

Several scenarios have been used in this book to illustrate the flexibility of this methodology. If this is your first step into personal development, you have a solid foundation to build upon. If you use other methodologies, strategies, and practices, then this work will only amplify their effectiveness. Why is this? Because you use language for all of it. Journaling, affirmations, and meditation are a few common personal development tools that people use. A common issue some people face with personal development tools is they are repetitive, and people experience a disconnect between the words they use and the experiences they have. For example, someone participating in meditation may complain that it isn't working for them, they aren't getting results, they can't quiet their thoughts, they can't sit still, etc. All these complaints and frustrations are expressed in language. Since they are expressed in language, we can apply this work to our messages and amplify the effectiveness of the tool we are using.

Equally important is figuring out which methodologies work best for you. To me, the work expressed and shared in this book can be useful for everyone, every person on this planet, no matter what language we speak, where we live, or who we love. Language is foundational for all human experience. That being said, communal, cultural, and societal norms shape our experience of life and can add to our experienced limitations. How do we work through these and build the life we want? I believe the typical experience of people is internal resistance, in addition to the external resistance people around them share or express. I shared this when discussing my visitation habits with my children and ex-wife. When you combine the resistance from others, the internal resistance of yourself (regarding those norms), and frustration with your personal difficulty in practicing your chosen methodology, you are more likely to experience struggle.

Life is full of compounding judgments and experiences. This work will not eliminate the complexities of life, but it gives you a methodology of breaking them down into manageable parts and empowers you to address them like you haven't experienced before. You may be able to see the work you can do in dealing with those three areas I mentioned. You may see the capstones you use for each area and the building blocks that you use for each. Good for you. And if you can't see them just yet, I acknowledge you for taking this on and encourage you to continue doing the work.

As your proficiency and mastery of this work grows, you will experience resistance from your automatic responses, from your friends, family, and community. Unless they are applying this work as you are, you will feel different. Even if they are applying this work, you will progress at different speeds with varying proficiency. Topics or themes you are passionate about, where you "know" where you stand on the topic, are not exempt from this work. I encourage you to take time to intentionally apply this work to those areas. Likewise, when you have applied this work and developed a more thorough connection with your decisions, you will face resistance from others who have equally passionate positions that exist because "that's how it is" or "that's how it should be." As you saw in my story, your experience with others may be more challenging at the beginning. But as I continued to apply this work, those around me experienced me differently, which allowed me to share what I was up to. In that way, the door slowly opened to where the impact of my work was experienced and continues to be experienced by my friends, family, and community. Their experience with me has changed how we experience each other.

EXERCISE 4

Dealing with pyramids as they arise is not limited to the present. We have recurring conversations and past decisions that we experience as powerfully as if they just occurred. There may be past incidents, conversations, and confrontations that are unresolved for you. They may deal with friends, family, exes, coworkers, supervisors, etc. First, you will identify the pyramids and dismantle them as needed. In this way, you are practicing your mastery of language. Yet often, this will open up new opportunities that you had not conceived of or could not conceive of before. One such new opportunity may be to create a new message and share that with the person or persons.

If reading the last sentence brought on a wave of fear, discomfort, overwhelm, or a sense of "I know this won't go well," I truly congratulate you. As we have discussed, creating a new world will come at odds with the world you are bumping up against. The first bump is addressing things in your life that you have not fully addressed. You may be drawn to engage with others to do this. Again, congratulations.

You will be surprised how positive some of these interactions will be. And you will be "proven right" when they are not so positive. Do not despair. Nothing in language is permanent. You will try, and it will have a result. The result will be the external reality. What you make the result mean is your internal reality. What I want you to really appreciate is that your new actions taken after you've done this work will likely move something that hasn't moved, or that you haven't had the experience of moving, in a new way.

Do not make the external reality mean anything. Just as with the quote from Martin Luther King Jr., the results of your actions will hit you, and you will instinctively want to assign meaning to these. Let us focus on negative experiences. You will be frustrated, annoyed, offended, etc. that the result was not positive or not what you wanted. This could easily lead to making judgments about yourself and about the other person. Judgments about yourself could come in the flavor of "I saw that coming," "I should have known they would react that way," "How stupid was I to reopen that door," etc. Judgments about them could arise, such as "They will never change," "They are the same stubborn, arrogant, selfish, horrible, etc.

person they always have been," "Why can't they get what I'm saying?"

The exercise is this: pause and acknowledge yourself for taking action to create something new. Acknowledge that you practiced mastery of language. Acknowledge that you have done something uncommon, unnatural, and powerful. Acknowledge that you took those actions, said those things, and reacted those ways. Just acknowledge yourself. After you are present with your own acknowledgment, thank yourself for doing the work.

You can use the following script. "I acknowledge myself for taking action and creating something new. I acknowledge myself for doing something new, uncommon, unnatural, and powerful. I acknowledge myself for taking those actions. I acknowledge the external realities that emerged from my actions. I thank myself for my choices."

Acknowledgment is not a judgment. However you may feel about what occurred, what you said, how you reacted, etc., it does not matter. Do this exercise. This acknowledgment is about the actions you took. It is acknowledging your part in generating a new external reality. That is all. It's acknowledging your power for creation. This exercise will help develop confidence in your wielding of this tool set. Whatever step you choose to do next is your next choice. And we will always have the chance to make new choices. And you will.

As you have experienced in your life and as we discussed in this book, self-talk is powerful. At no point is it more powerful than in the immediate aftermath of a message, discussion, conflict, etc. It is here that your mind can "run wild." "Running wild" is not a tool set, as we have seen. You may think the immediate aftermath gives you some particularly valid or truthful analysis. It doesn't. Language has no inherent meaning other than the meaning we assign to it. This is true at all times; however, it is hard to experience this in the immediate aftermath of what you would call a "negative experience." That is why pausing and acknowledging is helpful. It's a tool to help create space for you to feel whatever you are feeling and not delve into old forms of language processing. Remember, your old habits will never disappear entirely, and the more you practice, the more you create a space to apply your new tool set, the more power you have to exercise control over language.

Conclusion

Once Ildefonso acquired sign language, he could communicate with his original teacher, Susan, more effectively. They saw each other infrequently because she now lived a few hours away. Ildefonso didn't like using interpreters to make phone calls to her, so when she received one from an interpreter with Ildefonso, she was surprised. The call was quick and to the point. Ildefonso needed to see her. It was an emergency, and she needed to come visit him. Then the call ended. Susan was worried that something had happened. A second call compelled her to make the trip, and she saw Ildefonso at his work.

When she got there, he was happy to see her. His emergency was not what she expected. His emergency was to tell her, "No matter what, I am your friend. Even when you and I are old [miming being old with an achy back, cane, and long beard], I will still be your friend. Now I have to get back to work." And he went back to work. That was it.

Susan wrote, "While driving back on the two-hour route I had just driven, I reflected that Ildefonso had no idea how many words we use or waste in our lives, in a million conversations, sometimes practical, sometimes just for fun and distraction, but often shallow and pointless. Decades of observation without comprehension, and the continuing isolation of working and living with no signers gave him a totally different perspective on what is important and how to spend language currency."

You have learned the three major steps in language mastery. Step 1, receiving the message, is a simple, powerful, and ever-so-hard step because we itch to respond to messages. Our responses can be private or shared, but what we have learned is to pause before they emerge to give us the opportunity to be with the message. And by being with it, we can actually get it without our added judgments. With Step 2, processing the message, we learned that in the course of processing messages, we use amalgamations of internal and external realities that impede our ability to address the message. The separation of these realities empowers us to take communication to a whole new level. We have also learned to utilize the pyramid model to deal with and decipher these mixed realities to functionally empower ourselves. The third and final step in language mastery sets us up with an uninhibited ability to create without reasons, judgments, or justifications. Choosing for choosing's sake. And for when things don't go how you would like or go "wrong," you can pause and acknowledge yourself for doing the work, creating space for you to reconnect with this work and apply it anew.

The effect of language mastery will appear in all your communications. You will listen to any message and not be "reactive." You can process any message and see how your automatic response is composed of external and internal realities. You will deal with those first, if you choose to, before creating your response. All these lead to improved listening, thinking, and speaking. Practice with different people, different communications, and you will see the way you interact with people and communications will shift. The world as you know it will change because the world as you know it is made up of internal and external realities. By changing your internal realities, you change the world for you and those around you through the choices you make. New choices for the new world that you are creating.

As you have seen in this book, a created life has a very big impact on you and those around you. Your life will shift and change in unexpected ways. When these new creations/opportunities emerge, the pyramids you built over your lifetime will emerge; you cannot eliminate them permanently. Why not? Because they are built with language that is innate for us. But much like the professional athlete, your continued practice of the fundamentals in mastering language will allow you to quickly, seamlessly, and powerfully put aside or dismantle the pyramids so you may continue along your created path. We can all do this. You can do this.

I have shared the world I am creating in this book. I will continue to share the world I am creating online through my website and social media platforms. I do this for a very specific reason. We use language to create our world. And we all use language. We are all connected through language. In this way, the world I create and the world you create are connected. It is an honor to share our created world with you. I invite you to share your world so we may celebrate, support, experience, and join you in your world, as you have joined me in mine. Please find us online at www.nathanmaxosorio.com and on your preferred social media platform, and share your created life and read about the creation of others and myself. I look forward to hearing what you have chosen to create.

Acknowledgments

To my co-parent, Ivette Pichardo Osorio. Thank you for who you have chosen to be. Our children are very lucky to experience the mother you choose to be every day.

To my father, Michael Max Osorio. I keep learning from the choices you made while you were with us. Thank you.

To my mother, Laura Osorio, and sister, Jessica Lopez. Thank you for your partnership in the world we are creating together.

To my editor, Kathleen McIntosh. Thank you for your guidance and vision in what this book could be. It is only through your mentorship that this book is fully realized.

To my publishing manager, Katie Lathrop. Thank you for your support and keeping me on task.

To my graphic designer, Lindsey Bailey. Thank you for capturing my experience in such a beautiful and meaningful way so that it may be shared and experienced by others.

To you, the reader. Thank you for allowing me into your life through this book. We are connected. You, me, every reader of this book, every person on this planet. Together we are creating the world we want to see. Thank you from the bottom of my heart. Thank you.

About the Author

NATHAN MAX OSORIO is an attorney with over a decade of experience in private practice, focusing on immigration and special education. The son of Peruvian and Mexican immigrants, he is a passionate advocate for families, victims of crimes, and children with special needs. Nathan received a bachelor of arts from the University of Rochester with a double major in history and religion. A graduate with distinction from the University of the Pacific McGeorge School of Law, Nathan lives in San Fernando, California.

www.ingramcontent.com/pod-product-compliance
Lightning Source LLC
Chambersburg PA
CBHW030530080526
44586CB00011B/387